The Other Side of the Vail

by **Melinda Vail**

with **Ellen Weiner**

Dedication

This book is dedicated to everyone who believed in my work from the very beginning:

Jacquie Aiello, Karen Andrews, Marion Light, Anne Marie Pali, Char Roper, Gloria Rougue, Leanne Rowe, Nancy Wakley, Linda & Dean Webert, and Cathy Weyers

A special thanks to Matt Englehart whose hard work and determination have kept me on track.

The Other Side of the Vail

ISBN: 0-9747365-0-3

Printed in the United States of America

Cover Design/ Typesetting:	Nurhan Thompson www.redperfect.com
Printed by:	Biltmore Pro Print Phoenix, Arizona
Published by:	Melinda Vail, Inc. 4520 E. Indian School Road Suite 1 Phoenix, AZ 85018 United States of America www.melindavail.com

Table of Contents

Introduction
by Ellen Weiner

Blonde, buxom, bawdy - all in a five foot one inch adorable package - not exactly what I expected when I first met Melinda Vail. But inside this bubbly bundle is a woman who can connect to her spirit, enabling her to hear the wisdom of those on the other side of the veil.

As an intuitive therapist, Melinda has helped hundreds of clients receive confirmation about the transition of loved ones in order to resolve feelings of loss; assisted in the healing of many a client's inner child; provided general counseling regarding life's many challenges; and aided in the detection of energetic patterns that stifle growth. She has a no-nonsense approach to spiritual guidance. In other words, don't ask a question if you really don't want a truthful answer! But you might ask why should anyone believe what Melinda has to say? How is she different from other therapists? Does she believe that she's indeed special or was she *chosen* to dispense this information to the masses?

Melinda's clients regard her as gifted, yet her deepest desire is for us all to discover our own inherent gifts. She insists that everyone has the power to heal themselves, if only they would allow themselves to be tuned into the right energetic frequency. Her hope is to inspire you to take the leap of faith necessary to discover this power, or energy, within you.

To understand that Melinda speaks wisely from life experience, it's important to look at both her past and present. Though blessed with an amazing gift, Melinda is still a very real, down-to-earth person. She willing admits that she's far from perfect and still has her own work to do. She smokes, eats red meat, and her track record regarding love and marriage is not the best. For the record, her name is Melinda Vail-Gillette-Littlejohn-Kuhlman-Vail-Saine. She has three beautiful children, who she pretty much raised by herself, as well as being mother to two step-children. The astonishing thing about this very real person is that, unlike the majority of people, she has the uncanny ability to connect to her God-Mind, which allows her to connect to God's energy directly and receive information, intuition, and inspiration from God.

So how and when did Melinda discover her gift? Growing up in upstate New York, as one of four girls born to a blue-collar, Irish-Catholic family, Melinda's life was like others in many ways, but it did contain some twists and turns.

Being Catholic, God always played a major part in her life. Melinda recalls, "I remember going to church, not during services but during the week, when I could talk to the priests about God and also meditate. During one visit, I asked God to give me a sign that he did, in fact, exist. I no sooner made my request to God, when one of the priests invited me onto the altar. Now keep in mind, back then, priests were the only ones allowed on the altar. So, I took this as a sign directly from God and never questioned His existence again. From this, I learned that 'faith' is our greatest gift."

During her teen years, she experienced all the normal things most teenage girls encounter. Complete with horn-rimmed glasses, she probably would be labeled a nerd today. However, unlike most girls that age, she knew things would happen before they happened. This contributed to her sense that she was an awkward teenager. During one particular school day, she and her girlfriends were gushing over the most popular boy in school. She turned to her friends and told them that he would ask her to marry him one day. And he did!

As she matured, Melinda discovered she was clairaudient, which means that she can hear things while tapping into other people's energy fields. To watch Melinda at work is to witness a transformation into a being truly connected with God. While in a trance-like state, her body is infused with an inner light; her normal speech patterns are altered; and her eyes become fixed. She is able to relate facts and figures that she would otherwise have no way of knowing unless a higher power was conveying the information to her. At the end of each chapter, you will find exceptional stories from real clients, written as first person accounts, which relate this phenomenon.

When asked why she thought she was given the gift of being so in tune with her God-Mind or spirit, Melinda again reflects upon her own life experiences. She says it's all about attitude. "No one can have all the answers, but what one *can* do is refuse to live life as a victim of circumstance. When I experienced hard times, I simply put my head down and looked for a new way to burrow my way out of the hole in which I found myself. I didn't blame others or turn to my parents to bail me out. I simply relied on my inner resources and tried a little bit harder. Each time I conquered a new mountain, I moved a little closer to hearing spirit whisper in my ear. And each day, as I continue to do my own personal work, the voice gets stronger and clearer."

Her journey through life holds universal lessons and truths, which gives her great empathy in dealing with others who have had similar challenges. Later on you will read of Melinda's life, which illustrates many of the principles and concepts presented in the following pages.

Melinda, first and foremost, considers herself to be a teacher. A teacher is one who simply channels information to enlighten her students on various issues. A *good* teacher does not push her own opinions on students but rather entices them to explore ideas from a new perspective. At a very minimum, it is her hope you will gain an understanding of how energy works on this planet, what she believes God to be, and how patterns in our lives take root at an early age and tend to repeat themselves unless we realize their origin and correct them. If the ideas presented here inspire you to seek a more spiritual life, provide information to help you better understand your own current life experience, or if you come to believe that there is more to this world than your five senses can dictate, then Melinda's job will be done well. Some of the principles may ring true for you while others may not. Keep what works for you, and discard the rest. At the very least, she will give you food for thought and, perhaps, challenge you to think differently about how you see yourself and your lot in life.

Whether you believe it or not, if you are reading this book you have been drawn to its contents energetically. You are, in fact, a seeker of truth. Here is one of the truths I discovered as related in an account of my experience with Melinda.

Always There

When my husband committed suicide seven years ago, it felt as if I died too. The searing pain pierced my heart so deeply that I felt disconnected from everyday life. I would watch the world go by as if it was a movie, and I did not have a part. However, my two children needed my care, so I walked through life accomplishing necessary tasks. Alone at night and in the confines of my bedroom, I would incessantly replay life in my mind's eye like a bad film. Over time, I revisited this film less and less. Very slowly the fog began to clear, although not without some hard work and introspection on my part. And while I can discern some of the reasons why he thought he had to leave, I still could not reach a definite conclusion for he left no note. As with many suicide survivors, I felt guilty for being unable to pick up clues about his unhappiness and spiraling descent into that final darkness from which he saw no return. That need for answers brought me to Melinda.

Through her abilities, I was able to connect to my late husband. Melinda relayed the minute details of my life - a rash on my son's leg; recent contact with a friend with whom I had not communicated for more than a year; the name of a new doctor I was visiting after my appointment with Melinda; a new business associate's name; and so on and so forth. Someone had to be informing her of these details. What I came to realize is that my husband was still present, watching over our children and me. Perhaps he was not physically there for me to see and touch, but he was in my heart and in another dimension close by.

After the reading, I went home and talked to him every night before going to sleep. I would beseech him to give me a sign that he was listening - to either throw down a book or rustle the blinds. Not two weeks later, in the middle of the night, I was awakened by a loud thumping noise. The room was very dark, and, since I was in a deep sleep, it did not really register what had happened. I drifted back to sleep and closer to morning I heard a whistling noise. By this time the light was wafting in through the blinds, and I saw the dust cover of a book floating through the air. It finally dawned on me what had caused the thumping noise. I looked on the floor, and there was a book lying quite far from its proper place on top of my armoire. I laid back down to think about it and moments later I heard some clicking noises over the intercom. I jumped from the bed to see from where the noise was emanating. I looked outside for noisy trucks or cars rattling by, and I checked my children's rooms to ensure all was quiet. Finding nothing out of the ordinary, I climbed back into bed. About a half-hour later the noise reoccurred. I followed the same procedure but again found nothing amiss. I turned off the intercom and told my husband thank you for the message!

Now that particular book, *Chronicle of the 20th Century*, had been sitting on its shelf for over a year and has sat there for another two years since this incident. My entire house is filled with books and has been for the last twenty-five years, and a book has never fallen from its place. So sometimes you should be careful about the things you ask for. How could I not believe that my husband was sending me a message, letting me know he was close by and fulfilling my request for a sign? I felt strangely comforted by this startling turn of events.

My interaction with Melinda opened up the door for me to truly believe I had not lost my husband; he had simply moved to another dimension. How reassuring for me to know that death is only another stage of life and that our loved ones remain with us always - and not just in our minds and hearts. It has made acceptance of his death easier, whether I ever discover the answers to my questions or not.

God: An Energy Force

When people ask me how to understand God, I tell them you must first understand energy. According to Webster's Dictionary, *energy* is simple natural power vigorously exerted. Everything in the universe is comprised of energy - of positive and negative charges in constant motion. Today, with the advances in quantum physics, we realize everything in our reality is, in fact, comprised of energy in motion, including the chair in which you sit and the car that you drive.

Our spirits are made of energy as well. In order to realize our own spiritual power we must look at how we exchange our energy with everything around us every moment of every day on this planet and beyond. Our bodies are 'life support' systems for the energy of our spirits. Since physics teaches us that energy can not be created nor destroyed, but only transformed or transmuted (changed), our soul energy continues on after its current "life support" system, or body, is destroyed. That makes death, as we perceive it, not a reality.

It might be easier to think of it like this:

God is like the energy of an electrical transmitter. This electrical transmitter sends energy to multiple buildings and homes. Each building and home has multiple rooms. When a light is turned off in one room, the current is still there. The energy is still flowing even though the light has been turned off.

God is an energy force effortlessly reflecting all the life in the universe. Human beings are a conduit to this energy. Everything we think, say, or do transmits God's energy into everyday life. We are the 'light switches,' so even though our bodies may die, our light switch or soul energy continues on and remains a force in the universe.

The following three stories recount actual clients' encounters with this phenomenon. As discussed earlier, I have placed varied accounts from my clientele to punctuate the principles presented in each chapter. The story titles are in bold and written as first person accounts. It's my hope that by reading these you will understand how the concepts discussed can apply to real life situations.

Suzanne's Story: Mom, My Good Luck Charm

My mother was my best friend and when she passed away I felt I had lost my closest confidante. Although my belief system included the possibility of life after death, seeing Melinda gave me absolute confirmation that Mom is still with me.

With Melinda's help my mother was able to let me know that she has never left my side and that I can continue to seek her guidance when necessary. Sometimes when I feel lonely I will ask my mother to send me a sign, and moments later I will catch a whiff of her favorite perfume or another simple reminder.

Specifically, I asked Melinda if I would ever locate my mother's lost wedding ring. She told me that I would find it in a box when the time was right. Three days before I started a new job I found the ring in the back of a drawer, almost a 'good luck on the job' wish from Mom! My mother also informed me that she was glad that I had finally cleaned out the garage - something I had done the day before I met with Melinda. Although these may seem like insignificant events, it proves to me that a piece of my mother's energy remains in this world.

Denise's Story: A Mother's Protection

All throughout the animal kingdom mothers fiercely protect their young with whatever methods are available to them. My mother reached out from beyond her grave to save me.

Only sixty years old, not ill, and stating she was not ready to die, my mother was admitted to the hospital with baffling symptoms. In less than forty-eight hours, she was dead due to a mysterious heart ailment. Distraught, I sought out Melinda in hopes that I could communicate with my recently departed mother. I learned that she had reconciled to her fate and that she was happily ensconced on the other side where she had worked out her issues with her father who had died when she was fourteen. She said that she would be waiting for me when it was my time, just as her father had waited for her. Imagine my surprise when Melinda named family members, friend's names, and the fact that my mother was thrilled by all the roses that had been dropped off in her coffin during the funeral.

After this encounter hope started seeping back into my life, and I began to feel that life could be special once again. Carrying on, I scheduled a well-woman check-up. Thirty-eight years old at the time, I always exercised, watched my weight, and was rarely ill. I thought this would be a routine appointment. I, of course, mentioned my mother's sudden cardiac problems, and this alerted the doctors to probe further. Even though I was not experiencing any physical difficulties at the time, they discovered I had a significantly enlarged heart muscle. Further testing revealed that I had considerable heart defects and that there was a good chance I would need a heart/lung transplant in the near future. I eventually did have surgery, more as a preventative measure, for I could have been unsuspectingly struck down at any moment. I returned home from the hospital on the first anniversary of my mother's death. And it is she who I thank for giving back my life.

If she had not died, I would have never known of the possibility of cardiac problems. Since I was young and healthy and showed no symptoms, my heart problem would likely have been overlooked. And I, too, would have died at a very young age. Not that you can ever swap one life for another, but I feel my mother let go of her life to protect mine. Even in my sadness that she is not here today, I know how lucky I am for having had such a wonderful and protective mother.

Debbie's Story: Spirituality Released

I first visited Melinda on a lark and viewed the appointment as one that would be an interesting experience. What a surprise it was to discover another whole dimension to life, one I believed in but about which I had no actual proof. It altered my life and set me on many paths that I never even knew existed. It was truly the beginning of my own spiritual journey. It also confirmed that we are spiritual beings having a human experience and not vice versa.

My father had died seven years before I met with Melinda, and we tried to reach his spirit. Melinda told me "he was too busy to talk to me." My first thought was, "Well, that's a good excuse!" She went on to tell me he was getting ready to help Milton pass over. Milton, my paternal uncle, was in good health at the time of this appointment. Upon returning home, just to be on the safe side, I called my mother to check on my uncle. She confirmed that he was well. However, not a month later and on the Jewish holiday of Passover, Milton died unexpectedly of a heart attack. I have learned since then that when Melinda talks about people dying she usually refers to it as crossing over; however, in speaking about my uncle she very distinctly said pass over. I have to believe it was a reference to the day of his death. This convinced me that she was indeed connecting to those souls on the other side of the veil. Over the next six years, I returned many times for several more readings. She told me of my mother's death, almost to the exact day, two years prior to her passing. And I have also learned helpful information about my romantic relationships.

I found my readings fascinating, but the most important lesson I learned was how to unleash my own power and find my own answers. The way to this end was through meditation and the acceptance of self. I'm no longer fighting against myself, but instead surrendering to the situation and allowing the flow of the universe to lead me in the right direction. Through this new connectivity to the universe, I find that I have the ability to make whatever I want in life simply happen. I'm no longer afraid of the pitfalls I will encounter, for I know now that I am here to have a human experience and to learn lessons from these experiences.

God's Energy: A Giant Mirror

If you accept that everything in reality is comprised of energy, then imagine God's energy as if it were a giant mirror reflecting back whatever you project out to it. In this sense, and like a mirror, God is a non-judgmental force and is everywhere at once.

If man is made in God's image, then we are all ultimately responsible for what is created in our own lives. We still have free will; however, it is uniquely contained within each of our own destinies. Destiny is the design or plan (karma) that our soul chooses upon coming into lifetime.

Here is an easier way to look at it.

Let's say that you live in New York, and you want to travel to California. California is your destination or plan for your future. Your destiny (karma) or design is to see California. Your free will allows you to choose how you're going to get there. You could drive, take a bus, take an airplane, drive a motorcycle, walk, hitch hike, go by train, or travel by boat, etc. Each mode of transportation will have different experiences, challenges, encounters, hardships, and pleasures attached to it.

God's energy will ultimately mirror back the mode of transportation that you will choose to find your own spirit. People have free will choices in what they choose to project into the mirror that is God.

Here are some examples as to how your thoughts get projected to God and what their non-judgmental reflection back sounds like.

You say: "I need to lose weight."

God says: "You need to lose weight."

Since God's energy is holding no judgment, the use of the word need gets reflected back to you and you continue to need to lose weight. Since you focus energy on that need, it cannot be released.

God will always confirm your original thought or feeling and reflect it back.

You say: "I need money."

God says: "Yes, you need money." (Then your car breaks down)

It's really simple - *what we resist persists.* In resistance, we give energy to a thought or feeling, and God has no choice but to reflect it back to us. It is as if we have blocked the flow of God's energy so it can not be released.

Since the language of God is one of mirroring and confirming our own thoughts and feelings, we must learn how we communicate with God so we can understand how to create our own true desires.

The following two stories illustrate how each of us holds so much power within our own hands. We always have the free will to respond to our circumstances appropriately. This allows us to see the big picture of our life rather than becoming waylaid by seemingly disconnected incidents. There is a greater plan - your destiny; it is just up to you to choose which path to take.

Leigh's Story: Passing Over Gently

Losing my beloved mom to cancer within two months of her diagnosis was devastating. What made it easier was to see how gracefully she passed from this world to the next. On her deathbed, encircled by her family, Mom felt the overwhelming outpouring of love and affection we all held for her. Knowing it was her time, she implored us to just let her go. I will always remember what she said: "Your love is too strong. It's keeping me here when I long to go. I see your father and grandfather waiting for me. Please release me." And so we did, knowing that she was simply crossing over to a different dimension and would never be too far away from us. Moments later, she peacefully slipped into an everlasting sleep.

It has only been three weeks since her death, but I find myself still talking to Mom. During these times I want to believe she is listening, but I don't always trust my experience. I always feel an overwhelming sense of calm and love surrounding me. And it is not just that love for my mother is coming from me, I feel that love being reciprocated. I ask myself, is this real, or do I want it to be true so badly that I only imagine it to be real? I have decided that I am going to trust my intuition, or that silent knowing, and accept that my mother is still here watching over and protecting me just as she did when she was alive.

Melinda had foretold of my mom's medical difficulties during our reading. Peering at Mom's picture, Melinda's eyes focused on her chest area. She then delicately suggested that a medical examination should not be put off for much longer. I pushed to know if this was a fatal situation. Melinda would only reiterate that my mom should see a doctor, but that the problem was not in her lungs. Two weeks later, Mom discovered a lump under her arm. It was only then that she visited the doctor and found out that cancer had metastasized throughout her entire body.

Along with the information about my mother, Melinda mentioned various names and events. Examining the context of my life, they all seemed to make sense. I believe Melinda gives you a roadmap that is dotted with names, places, and incidents. It is then up to us to connect the dots and make sense of the big picture. And it is our free will that allows us to form the picture in any manner that we wish.

Leslie's Story: There Are No Crystal Balls

Death, divorce, loss of a job, loss of a house, loss of community standing - different types of losses, but they all take their toll on the human spirit. For some, it makes them grow stronger and more resilient, and for others, each loss weighs more heavily upon the shoulders until one feels beat up and downtrodden.

During these times of loss, one may feel uneasy about his or her place in this world. The world has tilted, and one must transition or change into a new person who is able to deal with these unforeseen changes. Sometimes I wish I could hurry through this transition and just reach the safe shore of the other side, but I know deep within my soul that it is in the midst of chaos where I learn my most important lessons.

It was in this chaos that I sought out Melinda. From early on in our marriage, my husband and I suffered tremendous losses - the loss of parents at a young age, friends dying, and a bankruptcy. With each loss, I reached down into my own personal well of strength and was somehow able to go on. My husband did not fare as well. Since some men define themselves by their work accomplishments, the loss of a thriving business dampened his spirit. This particular event was indeed a contributing factor to our separation.

When I asked Melinda if she foresaw a divorce, her answer was a firm *no*. Things had progressed to a legal separation, and I didn't know if divorce was in the cards. Melinda stated, "The future is very hard to predict, for one always has free will to reframe his own life. What could be true at one moment does not necessarily have to remain true. We each hold our destiny in our choice of thoughts and subsequent actions."

Visiting Melinda because one thinks she has a crystal ball is a silly proposition. Visiting her to learn about some of the possibilities that were not previously considered is a better use of her knowledge. Everyone possesses his/her own crystal ball because each of us ultimately has the ability to visualize what we want in our futures.

Accessing God's Energy: Our God-Mind or Divine Mind

Once we understand how God's energy works and sharpen our ability to tap into the mirror of God, we can then access the part of ourselves we will call the *God-Mind* or the *Divine Mind*.

Have you ever thought about where your mind is located? Is it a part of your body, or is it a part of your brain? Consider for a moment the fact that your mind could be outside of your brain and only energetically attached to your body, while technically not being a part of your body at all.

Since the brain is a fixed part of your body, how could *it* ever be changed? Yet we have no difficulty changing our minds, therefore your mind must be outside of your body. Perhaps we should think of the brain as merely a tool of the mind. Compare your brain to a giant computer bank storing experiences as data and sending information to different parts of your body. Think of your mind as being right outside and above your body, constantly exchanging information with your brain's computer bank to the universe.

If the mind is outside the body, but still energetically attached to it, this would allow your mind to be logically a part of God communicating through the energy of the universe. The God-Mind enables us to receive information, intuition, and inspiration from God.

All people are connected to each other energetically through their individual God-Minds. This connection is what we call *collective consciousness*. Collective thought or consciousness, in both the positive and negative, is a very powerful tool and can bring immense changes in all people's lives and the world at large.

The two following accounts reveal how, even though we are individuals, we are all connected energetically.

Dawn's Story: A Team Effort

I am a civil engineer who previously was working at a firm for quite a while with the hope that one day I could branch off on my own. At the time, though, operating my own business was a very scary thought. I knew I had the talent and wherewithal to be my own boss, but the loss of a consistent paycheck was certainly holding me back. I approached Melinda to seek advice on what I should do.

She told me that I should have the courage to step into the unknown and that the current need for my talents would soon increase. I would also be receiving a large work order from a man named Jack. Within three weeks a gentleman offered me a huge consulting job which was so large it would force me to quit my current job in order to fulfill the requirements. Nonchalantly, one day the gentleman asked me if I had ever heard of the financier of his project. Of course, his first name was Jack! So that day I quit my day job and began to work on my own as a consultant.

In addition to the new contract, Melinda told me that I would be pregnant within four months. My husband and I had earlier decided to wait another year before trying, but I found myself with child two months after my reading with Melinda. She told me the baby would be a boy, and, of course, it was a son who we welcomed to our family.

In the past, I had always felt that I alone was the master of my own destiny. In making both business and personal decisions I had always felt a gut emotion or some other inner tug in one direction or another. I just could never quite grasp 'how' I knew or from where exactly this information was coming. My experience with Melinda taught me that Spirit, or my connection to my God-Mind, is always guiding me. Of course, I still have free will to decide in what direction I will go, but now feel I have a partner to help me along the way.

Arlene's Story: The Skeptic

In my childhood household a chiropractor was looked upon as a 'voodoo' doctor. Take that belief and mix it with the Jewish faith, where our time on earth is emphasized as being the most important and there is no mention of an afterlife, and you have a pretty conservative view of the world. Imagine my own bewilderment as I now find myself employed by a group of alternative medical practitioners as well as having an association with an intuitive therapist! Being quite skeptical about being able to communicate with those loved ones who have passed over, it took a lot of coaxing for me to make my first appointment with Melinda.

I lost my eldest brother in a car accident when he was only fourteen years old, and I was two years of age. Even at that tender age, the gap made by his absence left a deep impression upon my soul. I had three older brothers - 10, 12, and 14 - but the eldest held a special place in my heart. And it disappeared in one moment when my mother's car was hit by a semi. The car flipped, my brother was ejected, and he was dead upon impact.

Although a little fuzzy in my mind, I still remember not understanding exactly just what had happened to him. After the funeral lots of people came over to our house to pay their respects. I remember thinking, "Oh, how nice - a party! But why isn't my brother here to help us celebrate?" Not being able to understand eventually turned to sorrow, and the sorrow slowly turned to anger.

My family situation was far from ideal. I lived in the midst of a hotbed of volatility where verbal abuse was the norm. My father and brothers never mentioned my eldest brother; it was as if he never existed. My mother, on the other hand, a compulsive chatterer, told many stories about him. But that is what he became -- almost a caricature of himself, invented by my mother's stories. Since I was so young, my mother's memories eventually became my own.

As I grew older, the dysfunction I observed in my own family situation became clearer and clearer. I was angry at the world, and, most of all, I was angry with my brother for leaving me. I blamed our dysfunction all on him. If he had not left, then my parents, siblings, and I would have lived happily ever after, or so I wanted to believe.

When I approached Melinda, it was my brother with whom I longed to connect and to discover if I could resolve my anger toward him. With her help, my brother conveyed to me that he chose to leave this world, but that he had been stuck at fourteen years of age because I would not let him go. My brother helped me to see that there was always dysfunction in my family, even before his death, so it was imperative that I stop blaming him for an unhappy childhood and to let go of my anger. I was still skeptical of these words since Melinda could very well just be giving me the advice that I needed to hear. However, when she mentioned the name of the street on which my brother had an appointment that fatal day, something turned inside of me. There was no way that she could have had that information without some entity, be it my brother or not, placing it in her consciousness. And so I became a believer.

Communicating with God's Energy:
The Whole and The Three Dimensions of Your Being

If we understand and accept that our God-Mind is always accessible to us, we must now learn how to communicate with it. One way is to picture yourself as a corporation. Our spirit, our subconscious minds, and our conscious minds are the three ruling partners of this corporation which make us up. Our *conscious* mind is the public relations partner - the one that presents itself to the world, and our *subconscious mind* and *spirit* are the silent partners. In fact, they are both so silent that sometimes we don't even know that they are there; however, they are the moneymen who hold the bottom line. In other words, they are the controlling factors in understanding yourself, and they have more direct communication with the God-Mind and the mirror of God's energy.

Since our bodies and conscious minds act as if they are not connected to our subconscious mind and spirit, communication with God is greatly misunderstood. This is why we may become confused as to why our life path is always cluttered, and the choices we make sometimes backfire. In other words, if we remember the previous example about choosing the mode of how to get to California, we can't quite understand why we are walking there instead of traveling by plane. We then question ourselves about why we may have chosen a more difficult mode of transportation to reach our goal.

To appropriately connect to our God-Mind and receive God's reflective energy in a positive way, we must first understand the language of our subconscious mind and how our spirit's energy works. It is important for us to understand fully how these concepts work in order to properly communicate with our God-Mind and then appropriately apply it to our lives. It is a matter of accepting a different worldview: that we are not separate, but rather a part of the whole universe. Our lives are not narrow, but in fact wide, and our opportunities endless if we are able to get in touch with that God-like part of ourselves: our God-Mind.

Read the following description of a man who did just that.

Mike's Story: Awakening

Growing up in a staunch Catholic and a so-so Episcopalian household did not leave much room for thought involving alternative spiritual matters. Nevertheless, at the tender age of ten or so, I started to question the tenants of the church and organized religion in general.

As I grew older I found myself experiencing many instances of déjà vu as well as repetitive, vivid dreams. In one particular dream, I found myself in a field that spans a great distance. The tall fronds of grass waved in the wind, while in the distance the meadow tapered off. I ran and ran through the field, yet I could never reach its end. I would wake up with the feeling that I was searching for something, but somehow it eluded me.

Perhaps this dream is a metaphor for my life. Rejecting organized religion, I read many books on spirituality. Over the years, I have always intuitively felt that there was a universal force that surrounds us all. It's not a force of good or evil, as the church would have us believe, but one that is always present and one that always allows us the free will to choose our own path. I have introspectively delved into my psyche to come to recognize that there must be another dimension that exists in tandem with our own reality. I have opened my eyes to the universe to accept that everything happens for a purpose and that there really are no coincidences. I also believe that there are some people we encounter that we feel we've known forever, and most probably we have - be it in another life or alternative dimension.

So from all these thoughts I developed a spiritual belief system, yet I still held a healthy bit of skepticism as well. I only had a *sense* that these things were true or existed. Somehow I still needed to tear down the wall I had built and find some way to actually KNOW that what I felt was true and real. This is where Melinda came in.

I was told that a first reading with Melinda usually leaves you speechless with your jaw left wide open. Since she can connect to the God-Mind, she can retrieve names, dates, figures, and events. As she transcribes them on to her tablet of paper, she confirms their significance to you. During my reading, a third of the information made sense to me. That evening I called my parents and rehashed what I had been told. They confirmed ninety-nine percent of what she said, including the fact that my brother was having marital problems (something that no one else knew except my brother and parents) and that my mother had had two miscarriages before I was born (a fact not shared with anyone but my father). I had finally received the confirmation for which I was searching. My burning questions about the existence of an afterlife, reincarnation, alternate dimensions and many other topics were also answered. I now feel more at peace with my place in the world.

Man's Grounding Energy: Duality and Ego

Communication with our God-Mind is a reciprocal act - that is, man is experiencing God while, at the same time, God is experiencing man. Consider the idea that man is the manifestation of God's energy in dense matter. God simply experiences itself in dense matter via our individual life support systems or, what we call, our bodies. Our soul or spirit, connected through our God-Mind, is the charge or battery for God's energy. Similar to a car's engine, which needs both positive and negative voltage to start it, the energy of God needs both a positive and negative charge to start the soul's energy. This concept is known as *duality* or the idea of opposing forces (i.e. good vs. evil, light vs. dark, ego vs. spirit). This polarity, or duality, is the energy that grounds us all and is created by human emotions. As God is a giant mirror, the world today reflects this duality within us all. One of the biggest dualities that exists is between ego and spirit.

On our planet, Earth, we live in what is called third dimension. In this dimension, God's energy is filtered through a veil called *ego*. The ego creates a false sense of self. The false self believes that God is totally separate from us and that we are merely bodies with brains.

Our emotions stem from our egos. Our egos are part of both our conscious and subconscious minds. They create judgments on both positive and negative emotions. Much of our ego is constructed in childhood and misunderstood by the subconscious mind. This is what creates the false sense of self. In other words, whatever we are taught in our childhood impacts our subconscious minds. These impacts are then retained in our egos and give rise to reactions we experience in adulthood.

The real self within our spirit recognizes that any events in our lives are neutral events, except for the emotion that we assign to them. Man must have emotion to gain insight and knowledge to learn about himself, but duality exists in finding the balance between the ego and spirit.

People whose tendency it is to spend too much time in ego remain stuck in their earthly agendas. However, by the same token, people who spend too much time in their spirit can be too far removed and so are not able to be grounded to their energy. Both types of people are, therefore, out of balance and need to realize the purpose of both the ego and the spirit for growth.

One of the saddest manifestations of being out of balance is the act of suicide. Learn from the following narrative that one's struggles do not necessarily end at the end of physical life.

DeeDee's Story: Useless Guilt

On the day my son took his own life, he also stole both his father's life and mine, perhaps not physically, but emotionally and mentally. Having just recently passed the one-year anniversary, it is still difficult to believe that my beautiful boy is not with us anymore.

He was our beloved child, the youngest of three. He was accomplished, well-educated, nice-looking, well built, and exceptionally bright: a true Renaissance man. He had everything in life to look forward to and a bright, shiny future in front of him. How did he spiral down so far into the depths of despair that he thought he had no option other than to commit suicide? How did I miss the signs? How can I build a life without him, for he has left such a large, gaping hole deep within my soul? Weary and grief-stricken, I felt an overwhelming desire to see if I could communicate with him in some fashion.

Although a bit skeptical, but wanting to believe it possible, I approached Melinda with a list of questions for my son. And communicate we did. I learned that he was surprised to find himself in the place where he was now. He always thought that death would halt his various struggles with life's issues. However, what he discovered is that once 'on the other side' you are held accountable for your past deeds. You must go to 'school' to learn about how different choices could have been made. He asked for our forgiveness, for it was never his intention to bring sorrow to our family. His suicide was about his inability to see the other options available, not his family's inability to offer solace and support.

What was it that actually made me believe that my son was speaking with Melinda's help? Amongst other things, she told me that he would send me an e-mail. Weeks later, I received a business e-mail message. Upon printing it out, I saw my son's name written on the top of the sheet. I looked back at my screen, and his name did not appear anywhere on it. I printed it out many times over and over and each time his name would appear on the printed copy.

Melinda, who had never been to my house, said she saw a blue glass bird in her mind. My son told her that whenever the light shines on it, it is a sign that he is close by. That bird sits upon my piano and above it are skylights. At certain times of the day, the light hits the bird and a reflection is cast on the wall. When I look at it now, it's as if my son is winking at me from beyond. She also saw a butterfly, and days later I went into my backyard and was greeted by a swarm of butterflies in flight. Again, I believe, it was a wave hello from my son.

Do all these things alleviate the deep sorrow in my heart and make me miss my son any less? No! Do they give me a glimmer of hope that his energy still surrounds me and that he is not totally outside of my reach - a resounding yes! What I hope is that he will become the man I always knew he would be - if not in life, then in the afterlife.

Harnessing Your Energy:

Ego vs. Spirit

We've talked about ego and spirit being the greatest duality of all. Let's understand why we need to be able to find the balance inside of us. Our ego tells us that we are separate from God and from one another. Our self-worth is traditionally measured by what we have versus what we don't have. Our ego also tells us that it is always about the right neighborhood, right car, right clothes, right job, right school, right education, etc. that makes us a cut above or below the rest.

In contrast, our spirit defines us by our inner qualities.

To find balance and harmony in life we must encompass and embrace both equally. One is nothing without the other.

When we talk about someone as having a big ego, it is usually meant as a criticism.

Let's not forget that ego can also be healthy. Without healthy ego we would not bathe or brush our teeth daily. Healthy ego allows us to feel motivated and successful. Material wealth is an extension of someone with healthy ego and not a measure of who they are. In fact, it's healthy ego that drives us to understand ourselves spiritually.

Unhealthy ego is the part of us that feels damaged or unworthy, useless or stupid, fat or lazy, etc. It is the 'false' idea of who we are, which is created by someone or something outside of ourselves.

Here's how it works:

When babies come into the world they love themselves unconditionally. They love to look at themselves in the mirror. They love the sound of their own voices. They love to play with their fingers and toes. They even love to play in their own poop by spreading it all over the crib or playpen and just have a great time. Parents then step in and decide to guide and create boundaries and judgments for their children. This is an important part of parenting, so we can all live in a harmonious and peaceful society. This is also all a part of learning about healthy ego.

Unhealthy ego is usually created as a result of generational patterns. For example, how can a mother teach her child self-esteem if she has none of her own, or a father teach a child to restrain anger if he is constantly losing his temper? Prejudices, rituals, superstitions, and fears are all patterns passed onto our children, too.

Additionally, there are deeper more subtle languages taught to our children as a result of the energy presented in childhood. Some of these subtle energies can wreak even greater havoc in adulthood because they are harder to define. Let me give you an example:

> *Mommy picks up Jimmy from day care. She has had a long difficult day and now has a headache. When they arrive home, Jimmy goes to play while Mommy makes dinner. Being a typical little boy, Jimmy makes loud and vigorous "truck sounds." Mommy says, "Jimmy, stop that! You are driving me crazy!" This translates into Jimmy's subconscious mind, filtered through his ego, that he is responsible for his mother not feeling well. What is the result? Jimmy grows up with the idea that he is responsible for other people's feelings. He emits out that energy like an electrical current and subsequently draws relationships to him where he is blamed for other people's issues. Ego then, in Jimmy's case, falsely believes that it is up to him to make others feel better. This has now become Jimmy's "subconscious language."*

The false ideas, created through the ego, are filtered and planted into our subconscious minds. These false ideas are at the root of what creates our difficulties in finding our true self as adults. Since God holds no judgment, those false ideas get mirrored back to us and perpetuate the original energy onward.

In other words, since we are all beings of energy, through our God-Mind, we are constantly transmitting airwaves or radar to those around us. We emit out an electrical current that draws to us situations, circumstances, or events that repeat the belief system created by our egos. That is why healthy, positive thoughts and actions create healthy and positive situations, while unhealthy, negative thoughts create unhealthy and negative situations. Our lives are a mirror of the energy of our thoughts.

In the following recounting read about a man whose energy was one of anguish and the ramifications for himself and his loved ones.

Mark's Story: And The Winning Numbers Are...

No one can know the depth of despair to which a person sinks when he is contemplating suicide. The black hole in which he finds himself gets deeper and darker as the days go by. Soon, even the smallest sliver of light is blocked from view. And then, instead of being frightening, the darkness becomes comforting and safe. It cradles and protects the person from all outside forces - from life and all the decisions, large and small, to be made. Eternal sleep and supposed freedom from worry beckon the suicide until he can no longer resist, and life is snuffed out.

Unfortunately suicide is a permanent solution to a temporary problem. And while over time the problem may dissipate, there are no do-overs when it comes to taking your own life. My brother made this mistake, and it is his family that is paying the price.

I was very close to my younger brother. We shared many intimacies about our lives, or so I thought. I knew he was unhappy about certain circumstances, but I truly believed he was working through his issues. What a total shock it was to discover that he was in such pain that he could only take his life to escape it. Even though I knew it was his decision to end his life, I still feel so guilty that I couldn't help him. Of course, what I have realized over time is that he did not want my help. I could only do my part, as he did his. I could neither read his mind nor comprehend that he would commit such an unimaginable act. What hurt the most was that I didn't know the reasons why he did it because he didn't leave a note behind. And that is what prompted me to seek Melinda's help.

Melinda helped me understand that my brother exercised his own free will in committing suicide. There were other options open, but he chose that particular path. And because of those choices, he must now deal with the circumstances that brought him to that moment in time. He must also deal with the hurt and sorrow he inflicted upon those he left behind.

During the reading, Melinda kept reciting a series of numbers. They meant nothing to me at the time, but I wrote them down and thought I would check with other family members later. Weeks later, while cleaning out my brother's house and disposing of his belongings I came upon a safe that I had forgotten he had. A light bulb went on in my head, and it dawned upon me that the series of numbers must be the combination to the safe. I opened it up, and there lying right on top of some other documents was a note addressed to me. I ripped open the envelope to read my brother's last words, which included an apology for having to leave and the absolution of my guilt.

Object Referral vs. Self-Referral

Object-referral, the projection by man of negative emotions onto something outside of himself, versus self-referral, the utilization of negative emotions to access inner thought and stimulate growth, is another example of duality.

Usually negative emotions are viewed as weaknesses, and so they are not appropriately dealt with in life. Yet each time we feel emotions like anger, jealously, or fear, we can choose to learn from them or not. It is the choices we make in dealing with these emotions, which determines the difference in the outcome of a situation. All too often we take these feelings and project them on to others. We say things like, "It's your fault I feel this way," or we stuff them inside ourselves by over-eating, over-spending, abusing drugs and alcohol, creating imbalances in our life, or having control issues.

This projection of our emotions, born out of our overindulgences caused by our egos, causes us to be out of balance and act in *object-referral.* Object-referral is when we view something outside of ourselves as the answer to feeling better about ourselves. Remember that the ego is created in childhood and stored in the subconscious mind. When we understand the language of our subconscious mind and how it was developed in childhood, we are better able to stay in what is called *self-referral.* In self-referral we can understand both our energy and the reasons for our emotions. We can then choose to respond appropriately to a situation rather than to instinctively react to it in the repetitive pattern we've established over time.

When we stay in self-referral we remain in the moment and do not get triggered back into childhood energy. A *trigger back* is when any given situation reminds our subconscious minds of a childhood situation with similar energy. When we understand the energy received in childhood, we are no longer triggered back and so have an easier time accessing our God-Mind. This way we can see the neutrality of the situation and allow the emotion to point us in the right direction of what we are supposed to learn at any given moment.

Consider the fact every event that occurs in our lifetime is truly neutral. We merely empower the situation by assigning a positive or negative emotion to it. Sometimes the only control we have over a situation is how we handle it; thus, it is possible for a seemingly bad situation to really be a wonderful opportunity. When the God-Mind is accessed it is easier to step back and see both the positive *and* negative aspects of a situation at the same time. By responding reflectively, rather than reflexively, spiritual growth is attained.

In order to accomplish this goal, we must understand our ego and our subconscious mind. This may be best achieved by learning to access our inner child through childhood regression hypnosis therapy. Before you try this, make sure that your hypnotherapist is qualified and knows how to properly perform regression work. Other ways to access our inner child are by writing in a journal, meditating, and participating in traditional clinical therapy.

Here is a simpler way to understand object-referral vs. self-referral.

First, consider that there are three types of people in this world:

1. Those who don't know what's happening:

    Acting in object-referral

2. Those who watch things happen:

    Acting in object-referral

3. Those who make things happen:

Acting in self-referral

Now let's look at these three types in the context of a golf game.

1. There are the spectators who aren't sure why they are watching someone chase a little white ball around. They just know it's great when they see a good shot or watch someone else triumph over a difficult hole.

2. Then there are the duffers. They are the ones who are not sure why they are chasing a little white ball around. They end up getting angry and frustrated, and yet keep hacking away at the game. They project their emotions and often blame a bad game on the course or the weather.

3. The last group is the professionals. They know why they are chasing that little white ball around. They use their emotions to gauge the game, adjust their swing or stance to the course, and to consider the weather. They know hitting a hole-in-one is rare, but they continue to strive to be their best. They are truly in self-referral.

The following is a story of how a woman wisely chose to respond to the challenges in her life rather than react with detrimental actions.

Jennifer's Story: Light At The End of The Tunnel

I was shopping when an adorable little statue caught my eye. It was fun, and I had to have it! It was not until I arrived at home and examined my purchase more closely that I realized it was a metaphor for my life. I had bought a "Woo" doll, and the attached tag read: *"The Woo is a benevolent force reappearing to remind us that a POSITIVE attitude is essential - that anything is possible as always with peace and love."*

In the game of life, I have been dealt cards from both sides of the deck. Today, I lead a fulfilling life overflowing with friends, family, a rewarding career, and time to enjoy myself. Yet I have also suffered many losses as well; my husband and two sons passed away within a relatively short time of each other. Although I eventually connected with all three through Melinda, each time I pondered how I would come to accept such unbearable sorrow. I also questioned if my well of strength would ever run dry.

The truth is that each of us has a never-ending supply of spirit inside of us that always allows recovery from despair. The trick is you have to make a conscious decision to recuperate and then allow yourself the time to move forward rather than remaining stuck in the mire of grief and loss.

At first, anger moves you through the cloud of distress - your anger at the loved one who has passed on;

your anger at the world; and your anger at yourself for not being mentally prepared for the loss of life as you knew it. So anger propels you forward with a purpose which allows you to deal with the business of life and to forge a new normalcy for yourself and your remaining family members.

Eventually you must resolve that anger and come to accept your new life. It is not better or worse - just different. You must begin to let laughter and light break through your cloud of doom. And in so doing, the wonders of the world are illuminated once again. This time, however, you are infinitely more aware of how precious each moment really is.

So having a positive attitude like the "Woo doll" does not mean that you are full of light and sunshine all of the time. What it means is, that despite the woeful situation in which you may find yourself, it is always possible to see that there is a light at the end of the proverbial tunnel. Tunneling your way through hard times, not around them or over them, is what really builds your spiritual muscle. It's also what ultimately keeps the smile on your face and the flicker of light in your heart.

Love vs. Fear

The duality of ego vs. spirit is echoed by the two core emotions on this planet: love and fear. All other emotions are footnotes to these two: happiness, gratitude, and trust are footnotes of love, and anger, greed, and jealousy are footnotes of fear.

While love creates our every desire, acting in fear will attract what we fear most. Fear causes a chemical change to take place in our brains. It activates the fight or flight mechanism. Many people live in this state of 'fight or flight' their entire lives. Once this chemistry is triggered, we stay attached in our ego rather than in our spirit. Since spirit is filtered through our minds, access to it is then halted. Thus, spiritual growth cannot be attained.

Victimization and complacency are companion energies to fear. Remaining a victim and being apathetic are two of the deepest fear-based feelings that directly interfere with access to the God-Mind. If we feel victimized or just don't care about anything, then we are not taking responsibility for our own lives and are completely in object-referral.

In order to access the God-Mind, we need to recognize and then surrender to negative emotions or pain. The emotions or pain must then be examined in self-referral to find the lesson that is being taught to us in duality. Next, we must take responsibility for these negative emotions while making sure we do not project or blame others for them. Finally, we must identify what is neutral in the event; respond to it rather than react to it; and use our God-Mind to help us express ourselves. Things are simple. We only make them complex. In surrendering to our negative emotions, we can then release them.

To better understand the concept of surrender, compare it to the birth process. When a woman is in labor she learns to breathe through her pain, or surrender to it, rather than fight against it. In so doing, the pain eventually dissipates allowing the birth process to become easier.

The following account illustrates how accepting and surrendering to a negative situation was turned around to be the best thing that ever happened to one woman.

Vivian's Story: Planting Trees

My life seems as if it has been an eternal search, although for what I am searching I am not sure. Perhaps I search because I inherently know that there is more to life than what exists on this planet. This belief system gave me comfort when I was diagnosed with cancer five years ago.

Up until that time, I believe I was uneasy with my place in life. I had dark dreams. I never could imagine myself as an older person, and I was unhappy because of many missed opportunities. When cancer descended upon me, instead of a black cloud of doom, it provided me with a newfound freedom. In my illness, I found the peace for which I had always longed. And when the cancer was finally cut away, my pessimism also dissipated.

Speaking with Melinda, I learned that my ancestors, particularly my grandmother, were still nearby watching over me. I was also able to speak to a loved one with whom I was angry because I did not get to spend enough time with him at the end of his life. She also talked about one of my older siblings who had an addiction problem. Melinda made me realize that it was his karma and that I could only play my part. I had to let go of my frustration at not being able to control the outcome of his actions.

Illness or personal tragedy brought with it a blessing in disguise; it made definite inroads in allowing me to let go of certain expectations. It also made me reprioritize because I recognized the fragility of life. After completing chemotherapy, I decided to get busy and make a meaningful contribution to society - perhaps not in a grand and showy way, but in all the little ways that count. I made a difference by counseling cancer patients and tutoring homeless children. And perhaps one of the moments where I touched their lives will alter the roads they take in the future. Most importantly, I don't feel any overpowering need to know how these people were affected by my actions. It is more than enough to know that I've made some impact on their lives for the better. As Nelson Henderson stated, "The true meaning of life is to plant trees, under whose shade you do not expect to sit." I've truly let go and in that process found my own answers.

Physical Energy

The Seven Chakras

We have discussed the concept of energy and the powerful role it plays in all our lives. We have also learned that we are, in fact, all beings of energy. Let's now examine how this energy physically moves through our bodies.

The human body, although containing hundreds of places of concentrated energy, has seven major energy centers called *chakras*, a Sanskrit word that means wheel. These wheels filter waves of energy through the channel of the mind to send information to different parts of the body.

Each chakra is associated with a specific color and refers to a specific organ in the body. The chakras also correspond to the seven stages of human development from birth.

Chakra	**Color**	**Location**	**Stage**
Root	Red	Base of the spine	Infant
Navel	Orange	Navel	Baby
Solar Plexus	Yellow	Rib cage where the ribs concave	Toddler
Heart	Green	Heart	Latency

Chakra	Color	Location	Stage
Throat	Sky blue	Throat	Puberty
Brow (Third Eye)	Indigo	Slightly above and between the eyebrows	Adolescence
Crown	Violet	Top of the head	Adulthood

Using the above chakra chart as a guide, you can learn to read a person's aura quite easily. Contrary to popular belief, it is not necessary to see a colored haze around a person in order to read his/her aura. The color of one's aura is constantly in flux according to his/her mood, so it is not necessarily an accurate reading of a specific personality trait.

A more accurate method is to see if a person has a 'break' or disruption in his/her aura field. A break would indicate the presence of some health or emotional issue. To identify a break, simply close your eyes and cover them with your hands. When you uncover your eyes, pay attention to where your eyes go on your subject's body. Wherever your eyes land first will indicate a break in his/her aura field. Consult the chakra chart and see what corresponds to the area where your eyes traveled first. For example, if your eyes went to a person's mouth, it could mean that the person has/had/needs braces or experienced/is going to experience another trauma around his/her mouth area.

A client states:

> *"Curious about intuitive therapy, I entered Melinda's office with a dose of healthy skep-*

ticism. I arrived with pictures of my family, and Melinda examined each one of them while checking to see if any of them had breaks in their aura fields. She took one look at my brother and asked about his lower extremities. She told me he was having problems with both of his legs and back and complications would eventually lead to his demise. He had, in fact, been experiencing many difficulties while walking and had had an operation on one of his legs. I don't really understand how all of this works, but seeing Melinda has certainly changed my belief system to now include the existence of a universal energy and my connection to it."

There is a thin line of energy running through the body, which connects the chakra roadway in a circular fashion. This energy line is called the Kundalini Energy. People who have had near death experiences usually report of moving through a tunnel or seeing a white light upon death. When a person dies, the Kundalini Energy (the soul) is released and travels upward from the root chakra out through the crown charka as a white light moving through the tunnel of its life support system (the body).

When trauma is encountered during childhood, it breaks the flow of the Kundalini Energy. Information regarding the trauma is then stored and remembered by the subconscious mind. This data is then emitted in the form of an electrical and magnetic current of energy. As this energy pulses and amplifies, it takes on a life of its own. The vibrational frequency attracts similar occurrences that repeat the energy pattern of the original trauma. In other words, adults find themselves repeating the same patterns and confronting the same choices stemming from the initial childhood trauma or original break in energy.

Here's an example of how this might work.

> *A young woman has been raised in an environment of abuse where she sees her father constantly berate and beat her mother into submission. She longs to escape this situation and grows up vowing to never place herself in similar circumstances. Unfortunately, statistics have shown that that is not what actually happens. In this woman's case, her childhood experiences placed a faulty language within her subconscious mind. She equates love and home with abuse, so she too eventually marries an abusive man and repeats the dysfunctional dynamics of her familial energy.*

If we can discover where a particular energy pattern begins, and also understand how it continues to cycle throughout a lifetime, then all states of disorder, dysfunction, and disease can be traced and corrected. Read of a woman who unearthed the core emotion that caused her illness to manifest and how she managed to turn around the course of events in her life.

Renee's Story: A Bump in the Road

Life was going smoothly. I had worked long and hard on all my issues. My children were doing well, and my relationship with my significant other had developed into a rhythm just right for both of us. And to add to all of these good feelings, there I was standing on the precipice of career success. All I needed was to take one giant step, and I was there.

Projects for which I had been networking for two years were all coming to fruition -- of course, all at the same time! Everything I touched was magic, and all that I asked for was freely given to me. What a wonderful situation in which to find myself!

Unfortunately, as some fairytale scenarios are wont to do, this one had one very big glitch! Me! Just as all of this was all occurring I found myself having mysterious physical ailments that seemed to have no apparent cause, or so the doctors originally thought.

I had many physical problems, and as I approach every dilemma with which I am confronted, I set out to solve it and make it go away. I was the most proactive I could have possibly been. I saw five different doctors along with specialists in acupuncture, massage, colonic therapy, and even a certified hypnotherapist. No matter what I did or who I saw, nothing and no one seemed to help. I was frustrated and mad at my body for revolting against me. I was unable to concentrate on my work. How could this happen to me? I generally took such good care of myself. I ate right, exercised, didn't smoke or drink, and rarely got sick.

Many believe that we, in fact, bring many of our own illnesses upon ourselves by our thoughts and actions and that these ills are indeed metaphors for our lives. Since there are seven chakras, and, each of these chakras relate to a specific part of our body, when we are sick one or more of these chakras are said to be out of balance with the rest. Since I was having digestive problems, it was thought that my solar plexus chakra might be blocked. By becoming ill, my subconscious mind was possibly telling me that I had bitten off more than I could chew which, in turn, caused a great deal of fear.

Now you might jump to the conclusion that I was simply afraid because I might fail. However, it was pointed out to me that it was actually the opposite. I was really afraid that I was going to succeed!

Consider the circumstances as mentioned above. Here I was on the precipice with so many options to pursue. Within weeks of different offers for work, I became so ill that I couldn't concentrate on my career, or anything else for that matter. Every day I went to a new doctor or practitioner for some sort of treatment. I put all my work aside and basically stayed home and tried to figure out how to make myself feel better. I tried to be patient with myself, and I looked for the lesson I was supposed to learn from all of this. I thought I had figured it out, but there still appeared to be no relief in sight.

It is only when I considered my fear of success that everything seemed to slip into place. If I were to become a success and be very busy, this would drastically change my current lifestyle. Previously, I had been self-employed and scheduled my work hours around my life. Taking that one giant step into the hustle and bustle of the outside working world would cause an upheaval in my simple lifestyle. It was a scary proposition, and, I guess, I panicked. My panic manifested itself in a nebulous physical reaction that the doctors are still not sure what it was or why it happened. It made me take two giant steps backwards and put a halt to my career advancement.

As soon as I figured out the why, I began to believe in a speedy recovery. I was still afraid, but I was going to move forward anyway. I somehow found the courage to face the unknown. I was about to start a new chapter in my life, and I think my body needed time to catch up with my mind. Emerging from my situation, I felt stronger, healthier, and had a keener insight into how one's emotional, spiritual, mental, and physical consciousnesses affect the circumstances of life.

Repeating Energy Patterns

Karma and Reincarnation

When a physical death occurs, the Kundalini Energy is released. Sometimes the energy of one's spirit, when leaving the life support system or body, has not learned everything it was supposed to learn in this lifetime.

All spiritual energy returns to a dimensional frequency that we call 'heaven' or the 'source.' There is no such thing as 'hell,' although sometimes we may believe we are going through it at times. When in heaven, our energy looks at how the previous life support system allowed us to learn and grow. After evaluating what was not understood versus what was accomplished, the spirit may choose to come back and resolve any energy left uncompleted.

We may not all realize it, but we always choose our parents (even if we are adopted), as well as the circumstances surrounding our lives when we come back into the third dimension (life as we know it). Karma, the universal law of checks and balances or cause and effect, is also a repeat of energetic patterns from one lifetime to another. Since we exchange energetic patterns from one lifetime to another, it is very important for us to look at our generational patterns. In so doing, it helps to understand the spiritual choices we made coming into life as well as the lessons to be learned. In fact, karma is literally a repeat of recycled energy left unfulfilled from when the God-Mind was in operation in a prior existence. In simple terms, it is what your mind "remembers" from a past life.

Here's an example:

> *I kill you in a past life. Most people believe that karma means an 'eye for an eye' or, in this case, that you will come back and kill me in our next life together. What karma really dictates is that when we come back, I will be given the opportunity to kill you again. Hopefully, the lessons learned during the past incarnation have been firmly imprinted in the soul, and free will shall be exercised to handle the situation differently and to not kill again, thus ending the cycle.*

The movie, "Groundhog Day," is an excellent example of how karma works. In it, the main character is given the chance to repeat the same day over and over again until he gets it right. So in this sense, karma is one of our greatest learning tools, since it deals with the law of conscious choice making. Every action we take, no matter how trivial, is made by choice. And every choice we make has consequences.

In everyday life we are constantly making choices, and the awareness of the effects of these choices helps keep our lives in balance. This human condition, where our lives are affected by challenges and decision-making, sometimes labeled by our emotions as difficulties, is what allows us all to eventually grow. By tapping into the God-Mind and by understanding and recognizing how energy works, all of life's difficulties can be overcome.

Read about a woman who did not know how to overcome her difficulties and how her choices affected those around her.

Chris's Story: The Power of Our Words

Interpersonal relationships are fragile entities. They must be gently nurtured in order to grow and flourish. Words spoken between partners hold the power to nourish, but, unfortunately, sometimes they are used to harm as well. This is the story of how words destroyed a life.

New to town and fresh out of a broken engagement, I met a wonderful woman with whom I was just having fun. I was not ready to jump into a new relationship, and she was in the middle of a difficult marital situation as well. Unhappy at home and not wanting to break up her family for her children's sake placed her in a no-win situation. We continued to see each other for five years and became incredibly close. During this time, she continued to be verbally abused by her husband but still could not free herself from the situation.

Eventually, she would have to choose to either stay with her husband for her children's sake or to divorce her husband and find the happiness she sought. The arguing never stopped, and eventually she felt pushed into a corner with nowhere to turn. Lashing out at him, she screamed, "You leave me no options! I might as well kill myself!" He said in return, "Yes, you might as well!" And so the energy of destruction was set in motion. She took her own life that day, leaving behind her two children, devastated friends, and me.

Wanting to end it all myself is what brought me to Melinda. A connection was instantly made, and Melinda could hear incessant sobbing from the other side of the veil. I learned that my friend realized that her death was a big mistake. Oftentimes, moments after the deed is complete, a person who commits suicide will say, "Oh my goodness, what did I just do?" But by that time, it is too late, for death is a permanent solution to temporary problems.

Feeling dejected with no place to turn, and, in an act of vengeance toward her estranged husband, my friend took an overdose of pills and drove out into the desert to die. Who did she really punish? It certainly was not her husband who quickly found another woman to replace her. In the end, her children were the ones who were punished by the loss of their mother, the same children for whom she stayed in a loveless marriage to protect.

Although my friend had a hard time communicating directly with me because the pain was so raw and new, what I realized was that she left this world with the belief that she was releasing me to go on with my life. I could never have deserted her, and she was too indecisive to ever make a choice between her husband and me. And even though she now may not be physically here at times, I can still sometimes feel her hand upon my brow, her arms around my body; and a whisper inside my ear. She lives on in my heart and soul. I am now stronger for having gone through this experience.

Reversing Harmful Energy Patterns

Karmic Energy and its Role in Reversing Disease, Dysfunction and Disorder

If the body is nothing more than the extension of the brain processes and a reflection of how energy manifests in the life support system, then all disease, disorder, and dysfunction are creations of the sum total. In other words, we create the illness in our bodies. This is usually achieved in one of three ways:

1. Through ideas created by the ego and filtered during childhood
2. Through our own subconscious ideas influenced by the God-Mind in collective consciousness (i.e. smoking cigarettes causes cancer)
3. Through karmic choices brought into the present life from a past life (i.e. birth defects)

The uncovering of our own subconscious language, or karma, is the first step in reversing a harmful energy pattern. It is only when it is understood and processed through the mind that a healing can take place. The mind can, therefore, change karmic data and its perception by finding the original language. God can then mirror back miraculous life changes to all of us.

Consider this analogy:

Every cell in our bodies vibrates with thought energy. This vibration can be thought of as a musical note. When the whole orchestra of the body is harmonized, we are healthy. When disease is present, certain cells are vibrating out of harmony or sounding off-key. The God-Mind or the conductor has to find out where the instrument is out of tune in order to recreate the sound of healing. If the conductor simply keeps leading the orchestra while it is still out of sync, then the tone of the body will always be flawed. After discovering where the original thought process created the energy flaw, then the God-Mind can access God's mirror and change the vibrational frequency, or sound, to one that is in complete harmony.

Age regression experienced under hypnosis is one way to access the conductor and find our original energetic language, which may be causing our bodies to sound off-key. Remember under hypno-regression therapy, memories are still filtered through the veil of ego. Therefore, it doesn't really matter whether a memory is real or imagined. What matters is that it is perceived and stored in a person's subconscious mind or body frequency and so can be the culprit which is creating the disease, disorder, or dysfunction in the current life.

We each create our own reality with our individual thoughts and our belief systems. Our thoughts are real energy and that is how we, as God-like beings, create. This thought energy is how we can also cause changes to take place within our own bodies. Since our thoughts and spoken words are sent out to the universe and mirrored back to us all, we can also change the world and affect each other as well.

On a grander scale, take into account the power of prayer. Prayer, through collective consciousness, is the most effective way to affect a positive change in this world. Conversely, through collective consciousness, we can also create disease and disorder that can affect us all. Consider the cause and effect relationship between smoking and cancer. There is so much media hype and worldwide attention to this relationship that our collective thoughts make it true. Yet there remain some people who continue to smoke who never get cancer. What could be the difference? Could it be that our own individual thought patterns create our own reality, or is it something else? And how does karma fit into the big picture?

Can soul growth then be the true purpose of karma? After all, man is what he chooses to be. He has a separate mind and free will to reframe his life and make new choices rather than staying stuck in old patterns. This knowledge, in turn, can lead to empowerment and the release of the disorder, disease, and dysfunction that plague his life.

The following is a story of a woman who, through age regression, was able to release various issues affecting her life.

Brandy's Story: What Do I Want to Be?

"What do I want to be when I grow up?" At some point in time, this age-old question is posed by both boys and girls worldwide. My whole life I thought I wanted to be a doctor until I began my last year of college. It was only then that I examined the changing face of healthcare. It seemed to be more about business than actually healing the sick. If I wanted to be in business, I could get a job right after graduation and not spend additional years toiling away in medical school. The real problem was if I wasn't going to be a doctor, what was I going to do with the rest of my life? I graduated and more time passed by, but, despite my expended efforts spent in unearthing the answer, it just didn't come to me.

In the throws of indecision and negativity about this state of affairs, I approached Melinda in hopes that she could send me in the right direction. She suggested an age regression to discover when and why my answer was blocked.

During the regression we tapped into the feelings of frustration caused by my lack of direction. Identifying these feelings allowed my subconscious mind to be triggered back in time to the original event. Since early childhood, my mother had always told me that she knew I was destined for great things. My perception was that if I didn't do something important my mother would be disappointed in me. Since all children want to please their parents, I tried to live up to her expectations. In my mind, becoming a doctor would be important enough to make my mother happy. Of course, the truth is that it was only my perception that was warped, and, in reality, my mother only wanted me to be happy and successful on my terms. Realizing that I had imposed these restrictions upon myself, I was able to release my indecision and choose any field I wanted to pursue.

The other major issue I dealt with during the age regression was the feeling of never having enough money or being constantly in poverty consciousness. Prosperity seemed to be a concept that was constantly eluding me. If I received a raise, the money magically disappeared and did nothing to alleviate my financial struggles. Since I held on to this feeling, I was regressed once again.

The first scene that entered my mind was a time when I was nine years old. My mother was on the brink of remarriage and assured me that once the wedding took place our money problems would be over. In my childish brain I heard 'Mom is marrying for money.' In my tenth year, I saw myself unhappily situated and ostracized in a new school, a move that was facilitated by my mom's marriage. In my twelfth year, the scene I saw in my mind's eye was one where I was playing with my new Atari game system that my stepfather had purchased for me. He wanted to take a turn, and, being twelve years old, I made a flippant remark to him. He grabbed me by the neck and in a threatening voice told me that it would be in my best interest to remember who bought me the system in the first place.

When I put these three incidents together, what I came to realize is that money had actually brought emotional and physical pain into my life instead of the promised security of which I had been told. I thought my mother only married for financial security. Since the remarriage, I was forced to go to a new school that caused me emotional turmoil, and my stepfather physically threatened me due to something he purchased for me. In my mind, I equated money with pain, and so throughout the course of my life so far I continually pushed prosperity away from me. Melinda had my subconscious mind realize that these two concepts are not intertwined and that I needed to separate them. So I did, and little by little, money, or the lack of money, no longer caused a problem in my life.

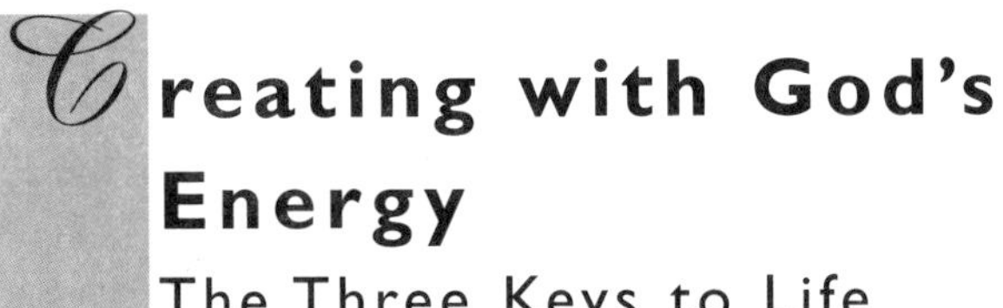

Creating with God's Energy

The Three Keys to Life

Energy is all about color, light, sound, and frequency. Once energy is understood, God is understood. Energy is carried through thought patterns, sound waves, and colors. Action is then required to complete the transmission of energy. This action is set in motion by using the three keys to life: meditation, affirmation, and visualization. Meditation, the first of these three, is what allows the stage to be set for God's energy to connect with the mind.

Meditation

Meditation, practiced in silence, is not as complicated, time consuming, and 'out there' as we might think. Those unfamiliar with meditation may also imagine people sitting cross-legged and silently chanting the word, om. While some people actually meditate this way, there are many other flavors from which to choose.

The easiest way to meditate is to close your eyes, shut your mouth, and breathe. In addition, you can meditate anywhere and at any time, even when you're exercising, walking, driving, or drifting off to sleep. Meditation is simply a time when you clear your mind of all the mundane chatter that usually fills each day and concentrate on your breath. It's a time when you can tap into your mind energy, which is really another way of saying the energy of God that is contained within us all. It clears the way for you to reach this energy.

As with any new skill, you must practice meditation in order to master it. At the beginning of your trials, you may not be able to make a connection or experience any type of earth shattering results. Do not give up! In order to reach success, you must practice it daily. What would happen if we didn't brush our teeth every day? Our breath would stink, right? Similarly, if we do not meditate every day, the same thing can happen to our souls. Meditation airs out the passageways and allows a natural link to be formed between our minds and God's mind.

If you are new to meditation, try the following technique.

- *Sit in a comfortable chair, close your eyes, relax your body, and complete the following ritual three times:*

    Inhale to a count of seven.

    Hold the breath for a count of seven.

    Exhale for a count of seven.

- *While you are breathing, make sure to concentrate on each breath.*

- *Feel your power as you slowly inhale, and then exhale your worries and concerns of the day away. Your mind should feel calmer and more relaxed the more you breathe.*
- *In this calmer state, look within yourself for any answers you seek.*
- *Try to let your conscious mind drift away, and this will allow your subconscious mind to surface. However, don't be overly concerned if mundane thoughts come into your mind. This is normal. Simply acknowledge them and dismiss them. Your subconscious mind is more likely to provide you with the answers that your conscious mind may deny you.*
- *Keep in mind that prayer is, in fact, talking to God, and meditation is when we receive the answer.*

Meditation is the airway to reach our minds. If we were under water, meditation would be our oxygen tank. Here in complete silence, accompanied by deep breathing, our energy roadways open up and allow our minds to work in harmony with every cell in our bodies. In meditation, we find fertile ground to plant the seeds of spirit and release the seeds of ego.

Affirmation

The process of affirmation is simply a positive assertion of thought. When we affirm, either in written form or verbally, negative thought patterns are reworked and changed to positive ones. These new thought patterns are then projected out into the universe, and, since God is a giant mirror with no judgment, they are reflected back to us. We simply need to realize that the circumstances we fear and the ones with which we have the most difficulty are exactly what we draw to ourselves. Like attracts like. If we let go of these misconceptions by speaking the truth and journaling away our fears (acknowledging them by writing about them), all the good things we want in life are there for the taking.

Remember to affirm all the circumstances you wish to occur. Make sure to make positive statements rather than negative ones, for example:

Do not say:

"I am *not* a cigarette smoker."

Negative

Instead, try these affirmations:

"I am a person who can breathe well and deeply without coughing."

Positive

"I am a person who loves fresh, sweet smelling air."

Positive

"I am a person who can exercise without gasping for air."

Positive

Always affirm with the words 'I am' rather than 'I will' or 'I wish.' This will manifest the energy that you already are what you are affirming, rather than what you *will be, wish* you were, or *will have* sometime in the future. The statement 'I am' brings the affirmation into the present.

More power is created when we verbally express or write down our own affirmations each day because specific energy is being used and put into action. In this fashion, our affirmations are reinforced when we speak them aloud or write them down as opposed to just thinking about them silently. It also helps us to feel more at peace with ourselves as well as help us to develop strategies to improve our lives. In addition to making positive affirmations, you might also try reciting the prayer: *God, be in my life and surround my life.*

Affirmation utilizes two forms of the God-Mind, the spoken word and the written word. The sounds created by man, through his spoken word and/or music, create a vibrational conduit to the universal energy field of God. Because thoughts are real energy, and words bring vibrational depth to that energy, each spoken word unleashes great power. It seems silly that man is moved by flowing language and dynamic speakers but cannot accept the depth of how his own words affect his own life.

Visualization

Visualization is the technique of forming mental images by using the imagination. Earlier we established that the mind is really outside of the brain and body; therefore, visualization allows us to form a picture in our minds and then pull that picture into our brains to digest.

Every thing in this universe was first borne in someone's imagination. Telephones, airplanes, cars, and the clothes we wear: all of these were first imagined before they were created. So we, too, can create what we desire. Visualize it; affirm it verbally or in writing; and then meditate on it. Opening up our hearts and minds allows the miracle of God's energy to flow through us, and we can manifest anything we want.

Visualization used with imagination is the most powerful of the three keys of life. All greatness is imagined greatness first. It is a healthy ego that propels us into great accomplishments. New records in sports are broken are broken every year, which is proof to man that even our bodies offers no true limitations.

Meditation, affirmation, and visualization used on a consistent basis are capable of helping to release the negativity and turmoil found in each of us and, in so doing, inspire us to live up to our greatest potential. In my life story, following, I will illustrate how I accomplished my goals by following these three keys to life.

Recognizing Your Own Energy

The Melinda Vail Story

I am a newlywed for the fourth time! This is the story of how I, Melinda Vail, at the age of forty-six, finally found happiness and the man with whom I wanted to spend the rest of my life. I am going to share my life story with you and show you why it took me so many years to stop repeating destructive patterns. It is my fervent hope that as you read my story, you can then begin to reflect upon your own life and figure out which twists and turns brought you to this moment in time. And if you're not currently happy in this place, it can show you how to begin to change.

Life is a journey full of many experiences and each experience, whether or not it's labeled good or bad, affords us gifts if we are willing to listen and learn from the experience.

As early as grade school we are taught that history repeats itself. Well, the same is true on a personal level. If you do not recognize mistakes and roadblocks you, yourself, have thrown in the way, your own personal history is also doomed to be repeated.

However, the belief system that I am presenting to you is not all about blame. You can not take your finger and point it at others and say it's their fault. Blame or responsibility for your life always rests on your shoulders. You may have found yourself in less than desirable situations at times, but it's your mission in life to figure out how to turn your disaster into a triumph. As with everything in life, this process must be accomplished by taking baby steps. But remember to turn around every now and then to see how far you've come.

In order for you to understand your current family dynamics and why you react or respond to the world the way you do, you need to examine the dynamics of your childhood home life. Let's first examine my life as a means of how to find the patterns, which are ones that may also run throughout other people's lives.

As you read the following story of my life, I imagine you may start to think, *"This woman has more problems than I do! Why should I listen to her?"* In collective consciousness, we want people in power, such as our political leaders, to be free of flaws. We also may think that clairvoyants or intuitive therapists know all the answers, so their lives should be perfect and problem-free. In both instances, this is not true. Leaders and followers alike are prone to imperfections in their lives. The difference is in how people respond to their own shortcomings. It took me many years and many marriages to understand my own karmic energy - why I drew certain situations to myself and why I seemed to repeat the same mistakes over and over again. I am not infallible. I have encountered many of the same issues that you find yourself facing right now. It is only when I looked at the reasons behind my actions that I could begin to understand how the same pattern kept emerging. I cannot change my karmic energy. I radiate out the vibrational field found deep within me. What I *can* change is how I respond to the situations that are continually drawn to me. And each time I counsel someone, I end up learning something new about myself and discover a different approach to a particular issue.

Early one morning and late in the summer of 1954, I was welcomed into the world by my middle-class blue-collar family. I was the third girl in a family that would eventually add one more daughter. I never really knew that we were blue-collar because my mother always taught us that we were better than everybody else.

What we are taught as children remains with us, in some fashion, throughout life.

This early lesson taught still lingers in my consciousness, and I occasionally find myself feeling superior to others. When this occurs, I find it necessary to watch my judgments and condescending ego.

In retrospect, I now realize that my mother's outward feelings of superiority, and the subsequent teaching of it to us as children, emanated from her deep level of insecurity and feeling of unworthiness about herself. As my personality and subsequent reactions to the world were dictated by my familial experiences, so were my mother's dictated from her own familial experiences.

My grandmother was the eldest and the only girl in a family of seven. Losing her mother when she was only sixteen, my grandmother was left to take care of her six younger brothers. When she married and set up her own household, her younger brothers and her widowed, alcoholic father came along as part of the package. My grandparents, being good Catholics, proceeded to start a family of their own with my mother taking her place as the eldest of six children. She somehow got lost in the middle of twelve children, especially because my grandmother consistently put her brothers before her own children. Coupled with the fact that one of my mother's uncles molested her as a young child, the feeling of unworthiness was borne along with some deep-seated anger toward men.

We have generational patterns that create memories in our cells.

As my mother was a victim of molestation, I encountered a similar situation with a neighborhood boy when I was ten years old.

It's a like-attracts-like-world.

Consequently, I draw many molestation victims to me in my hypnotherapy practice. Young molestation victims carry around with them heavy wounds to their souls. Usually there is a mixture of emotions, with shame and guilt heading the list. In order to move forward in life, the inner child must first be healed.

A miracle is simply a change in our perception.

As a child, I would frequently stop by my local church on the way home from school. I didn't know the term for it then, but I would just sit and meditate in one of the pews. As much as I enjoyed being in church by myself, my mother claims I would constantly refuse to attend mass with the family. So at the tender age of eight, I was already objecting to organized religion. However, I would still go to church by myself quite often to just think and pray - my own child-like form of meditation.

Meditation is one of the three keys to life.

When I did go to mass and listen to the Bible stories, I would visualize myself with Jesus in whatever story was being told. Occasionally, I imagined I was Joan of Arc or one of the children of Fatima. I'd also look into the sky at times and try to form the faces of Mary and Jesus in the clouds.

Visualization is one of the three keys to life.

I had an imaginary friend as a child, and her name was Stonny. I could see Stonny as a beam of light and genuinely feel her love for me. I know now she was my guardian angel. My mother always set an extra place at the table for Stonny. Most importantly, my mother never negated Stonny and always allowed her to be with us. My mother taught me that speaking to Stonny in public was okay to do.

> ***We stifle clairvoyance in our children by not recognizing or accepting that our children are actually seeing or hearing an otherworldly presence.***

Although on the surface I was the good girl in the family, underneath that facade I seethed with rage. I was very passive aggressive and partied a lot in high school. There was a lot of drinking and a lot of marijuana, but I was too much of a sissy to do hard drugs. I wondered if my parents ever knew because they never said anything to me about it. What I do know is that my angels were around me even then because I drove while impaired and somehow always managed to reach my destination safely.

One time I ran away from home. The only reason my mother knew I was gone was because my Virgin Mary statue and my pictures of Jesus and Mary were missing. A friend and I decided to hitchhike to Maryland to visit another friend's brother. The incident is very foggy in my memory because I believe I choose not to remember it clearly. I'm sure I could remember all of the details under hypnosis, but I have yet to do it. I'm no different than anybody else on this planet; I still have my own work to do as well.

If we think we are done with our work, we are in ego and create more karma.

As far as I can now remember, we hitched a ride in a semi truck and made it as far as New Jersey before we were arrested. In retrospect, I thank God that the police came along when they did because we were just about to be picked up by a man in a Cadillac. I didn't see the driver, but I remember having an "icky" feeling about it. Again, an angel or guide saved me.

I was arrested and spent the night in a holding room, a cement-walled room with no windows and just one door. It was not actually a jail cell, but it sure felt like one. We were charged with hitchhiking, running away, possession of a prescription drug not belonging to either one of us (it was my sister's), and the possession of a hunting knife that one of the boys from home had given us for protection on the road. Together, my parents and my friend's parents drove down to New Jersey to pick us both up. I don't have a clear memory of the ride back home either. All I remember is that it was silent.

After this incident, my mother stopped speaking to me altogether, and my father could think of nothing to say to me. Wow! What a punishment! My parents were giving me the silent treatment. I really did feel guilty, yet ironically enough I was very angry because it seemed to me that they thought that I was not worth punishing or at least deserving of a good tongue-lashing. I almost wished they would at least yell and scream to validate the fact that they cared. As an adult, I now realize that my parents only did what they thought was right at the time. I also recognize that when you see your patterns and understand the language of your energy, it's not all about blaming your parents. It's about understanding and taking responsibility for your own actions and behavior. It is about responding properly and not reacting.

Until I learned to respond and not react, I took this incident and parlayed it into a pattern that I repeated in all of my future romantic relationships. I have the tendency to push the man I love into proving that he loves me. For me, this recreates that inner child longing for someone to care enough to get mad at me.

> ***By healing your inner child and recognizing what your spirit has chosen to learn in this lifetime, you can learn to be responsive rather than reactive.***

My sisters were also affected by our family dynamics. In our small upstate New York town my two older sisters were known as the *Vail girls*. They were the popular cheerleaders, and, at age ten, I was the high school mascot, the Vestal Golden Bear. Who could want anything more? It didn't seem to me then that our family was so dysfunctional. We only knew our own family truths.

One of those truths was about my father. We knew we always had to wake him up gently and cautiously. I thought it was because he had been in the war. I knew that he had been in Australia, but I'm not sure how much action he really saw because he never talked about it. We just knew that his hair had turned white by age twenty-six, and I grew up with the *mistaken* impression that he had an earlier nervous breakdown or was shell-shocked.

Childhood impressions are true memories even if they are not completely accurate. They are true to the grown-up who remembers the incident through the eyes and the ears of the child he or she once was.

I always believed that my father must have been scarred by the war. He was depressed, on Librium, and constantly complained about his health. He had "the" stomachache, "the" headache, etc., always using "the" in front of his ailments to give them substance. We spent some vacations where he wouldn't even come out of the hotel room. In response, my mother's energy was one of intolerance, not in her words, actions, or deeds regarding my father, but in her energy. I knew she was unhappy and only tolerated him.

> ***My father taught me men were needy and weak. My mother taught me men were only to be tolerated. I have repeated this "truth" that I learned in my childhood in all of my marriages.***

Whenever my father was at home he would just lie on the couch and watch television, eventually falling asleep in front of it. My mother, on the other hand, would simply go to her room. In his early forties, my father started to have heart problems. These problems only made my mother more aware of her unhappiness, since a good Catholic girl would never leave a sick man.

My father used his energy with my mother to gain attention. Two of my sisters identified with my father, and they manifested similar energy. They were always sick or hurt and also quite accident-prone.

Not knowing very much about my father's family background, I'm not sure what caused him to exchange energy in the manner he did. This is not to say that my father was all bad. With duality in mind, no one is either all good or all bad. My father did have some really wonderful qualities as well.

He was very generous, and we knew he loved us very much. To this day, Christmas remains a major event in my family because my father managed to make it a very special time for all of us. My perception of my father was that he was a genuinely honest man with high ideals. It's ironic because most manic-depressive people usually embellish the truth and believe their own fabrications which, in turn, creates their own truth. However, this is not how I remembered or perceived my father to be.

I remember a time when my father told me that his bowling team had lost because someone else had misinterpreted the rules. Dad set out to prove his team had won and made several people angry in the process. It was a big "to do" in our household, but through this incident my father taught me to stick to your principles when you know you're right. In my family dynamics, my parents exchanged energy in a certain pattern, which filtered down into their children's fields of energy.

Children learn by the "language" of their parents.

So in their innocence, my sisters became what they saw at home. Two of my sisters, as adults, have been diagnosed as manic-depressives or having bipolar disorder. Although not a popular diagnosis in my father's era, I believe that he, too, would have been identified as manic- depressive.

Remember that it's a like-attracts-like world.

Alcoholism, ADD, ADHD, and bipolar disorder have similar energy dynamics.

One of my sisters and her husband (whose mother was mentally ill and tried to commit suicide several times) have three children. Their marriage ended in divorce brought on by chaos, drama, and eventual marital cheating.

Another sister has one child, and her marriage also ended in divorce. Her husband was a violent man and eventually committed suicide after the marriage ended.

And lastly, another one of my sisters married a child of an alcoholic with whom she has two children. Although her marriage lasted the longest, she and her husband finally divorced after twenty years. Over the years, she manifested multiple illnesses, including bipolar disorder and anorexia.

Despite the challenges each of my family members have had, I am still very proud of them all.

We have all joined together on a very powerful journey to understand our duality here. When properly understood, all of the things we have manifested can catapult us into enlightenment. And since this a like-attracts-like world, my practice draws to me alcoholics, those with bipolar disorder,

> ***relatives of those with bipolar disorder, people with eating disorders, and suicide survivors.***

So here I was growing up in the midst of all this chaos. Throughout my childhood I recall my sisters following in my father's footsteps by constantly vying for my mother's attention. In order for me to have a turn, I was subconsciously programmed to compete with them to gain her attention.

> ***I, therefore, have always drawn men to me that have energy attachments to prior women. This repeats my childhood energy dynamics of "competing" for attention.***

I married my first husband when I was just eighteen years old. He was a child of an alcoholic (COA), just like my grandmother and my mother, and he still harbored feelings for his high school sweetheart. Since he was a COA and I was a child of a manic-depressive, we were a match made in heaven! To complete the picture, he also provided me plenty of fodder for my competitive spirit. He had learned from his sexually unfaithful father that men were not expected to remain true to their wives. So he cheated on me, and I continued to compete for his affection.

In the midst of our eleven-year marriage, another one of my childhood languages reared its ugly head. Since I grew up with a father who gained attention through illness and since I had such a competitive spirit, I manifested several illnesses, including cervical cancer, a miscarriage, and a gallbladder problem which required surgery. I was also told that I would never be able to bear children. Of course, this pronouncement was unacceptable to me, so I just ignored it. Amazingly enough, we managed to produce three beautiful children, two boys and a girl, all of which were born by Cesarean section. I still continued to have health problems though. For three years in a row, from 1979 to 1981, I found myself in the hospital every July, either having a baby or having an operation.

Coupled with this stress coming through my subconscious childhood data, my husband also brought to the marriage *his* childhood poverty consciousness. His parents always lived hand-to-mouth, and he worked throughout his high school career to make the family car payment. So what did this do to our marriage? A sickly wife, three young children, and no money eventually led to its destruction. When my youngest child was three months old, I walked away from the marriage.

> ***The marriage had left its imprint in bold bright letters: love equaled pain.***

At that point in time, I wasn't able to tap into my God-Mind nor could I learn from my mistakes. All I knew was I no longer wanted to be in pain. Within months after my divorce from this man, I married another one who was a genuinely nice guy. Actually, he was a little too nice for me. I was not in love with him, as I had been with my first husband, but I thought a peaceful and stable environment would be enough for my children and me. He did, however, have his own issues. He was abandoned by his mother at an early age and was raised by his grandmother, father, and a very bitter stepmother.

His family circumstances made his language focus on women.

The women he encountered romantically were either too difficult like his stepmother, or they abandoned him like his mother did so many years ago. And, of course, I repeated this pattern for him. Our marriage was short and sweet. He was too nice and too functional for me, two personality characteristics that were outside of my comfort zone. I felt at home in the midst of dysfunction, but unfortunately I hadn't yet learned how to respond properly to it. I was still in a reactive mode that made a successful romantic relationship almost impossible. So in my twenty-eighth year, I divorced my first husband, married my second husband, and divorced my second husband.

I left my second husband for a clairvoyant. To me, this clairvoyant was the most fabulous person I had ever met. He knew things before they would happen, and he even channeled information too. To me, the channeling was wondrously frightening and charismatic at the same time, but I still found it hard to swallow. This man was by most standards unattractive, but, somehow, I thought he was the sexiest man alive. Simply put, he seduced me.

> ***Sexual energy and psychic energy are the same energy. It is all about passion, creative flow, and surrender into emotion without ego.***

In this relationship, I continued to repeat my energetic pattern of competition with other women. This man was a womanizer, and I got very hurt. And to add insult to injury, he was also seducing my cousin's live-in girlfriend.

> ***Just because a man can connect to and tap into the God-Mind, it does not make him any less vulnerable to earthly ego. This, I now recognize, was my lesson here.***

So I moved away and became associated with another group of psychics. There were three men, and they were definitely out there. Two of them were life partners, and the third was married. I went to their classes and learned a great deal. I found them all so strange and full of ego, since they all liked to compete with each other.

I wanted everything to be so real that I did not listen to my body when it said to run away from these people because something was terribly wrong. It took a little time and a meeting with a very spiritual lady to recognize my misguided beliefs. As confirmation, years later I found out that the married channeler had molested my oldest son. This again was a repeat of generational patterns, for both my mother and I were both molested at a young age.

Contrary to the psychics that I had previously come in contact with, my spiritual lady was everything one is supposed to be when working as a clairvoyant. She was accurate, caring, maternal, sweet, and, at the time, 'all knowing.' I thank God for her, for we connected and she took me under her wing. She was a hypnotist, and we worked to heal my inner child and clear my past lives. I wanted to be just like her.

> ***There is duality on this planet in all things, and we need to recognize that there is nothing here that is all good and nothing here that is all evil. There just "is".***

After divorcing my second husband and the interlude with the psychics, I struggled financially to give my children what they needed to survive. I worked like a dog, and one year I even held down four jobs at the same time. I sold advertising nine to five every day; taught diet classes three nights a week; worked as a waitress two nights a week; and was a hostess on Saturday and Sunday mornings. It was hard on all of us so my eldest son, who was eleven at the time, became the rock for my younger children who were then four and six. It was a very tough time with lots of struggles, lonely Christmases, no money, and an existence based on sheer determination.

I am sure these circumstances and memories have become a part of my children's language as adults.

After five hard years of struggling by myself, and with no real help from my children's father, I met my third husband. His family was of German descent. They were dairy farmers who kept their Lutheran faith firmly intact. These people sincerely walked their walk and lived their values, and I respected them for that. Their son, the black sheep of the family, was an entirely different matter.

He fit right into my energetic pattern, and his energy was such a comfort to me! Shortly after we met, he hurt himself on the job. I offered to move in with him so I could help him recover.

After all, as a child I had learned that sickness goes hand-in-hand with love and family.

He was also still connected to his former wife. She had broken his heart during their marriage, and he still wasn't fully recovered.

This played perfectly into my pattern of being in competition with other women.

During this marriage my new husband forged a bond with my second son. As a youngster he had wrestled in school but had not been particularly successful at it. When my son was seven, my husband set out to make him a wrestling champion. He and my son traveled to wrestling meets throughout the state. This bond was one of the things that I came to count on in our marriage.

However, this marriage was not meant to last either. Since it was not built on the sturdiest of foundations, it crumbled when hard financial times hit us. In fact, it was so bad that we were forced to declare bankruptcy. My husband was so depressed by this that he ended up on medication. I responded in a similar fashion and needed another operation, a hysterectomy. We persevered for a while longer, and, during this time, I was able to earn my real estate license while my husband delivered pizzas.

One day my husband was scheduled to take my son to a wrestling meet. He never showed up. After three days and no word from him, I started to suspect foul play. I contacted the police, and they eventually located him in New York City, supposedly with his girlfriend. This would have been bad enough, but the girlfriend instead turned out to be a prostitute. Outraged, I packed up his belongings and brought them over to his sister's house. I then packed my belongings, as well as my children's things, and placed a 'For Sale' sign on the front lawn. We then all jumped into the car and headed to Arizona.

Over time, my husband and I began to communicate again. He eventually moved to Arizona, found a job, and we attempted to reconcile our relationship. But it was not meant to be, and after eight years I became a divorcee once again. My track record was not looking very good with a string of bad marriages, financial losses, and family baggage.

Not one to let these things hold me back, I proceeded to make a fresh start for my family. I began to work with and recognize my real self: the little girl with the God connection. I tapped into that connection and found my God-Mind. I began to understand energy and the languages I had been carrying around with me. I began to surrender to the draw I always felt toward Spirit and became a conduit to it. I started giving readings that felt miraculous and learned that I could communicate with those who had crossed over. I meditated, visualized, and affirmed my true self. I let go of my poverty consciousness and became financially stable and successful. I became happy with myself again and that's when I met my fourth husband, Dick. Call it chemistry or whatever you want, but our karmic energy vibrated out to each other. Our lives seemed to have run in a somewhat parallel course up until this time.

- He has a brother with bipolar disorder; I have two sisters afflicted with the same.
- He was a high school wrestling coach; my son was a wrestler.
- Both our families had a summer cottage by a lake.
- We had both worked in sales.
- He had been married four times including once to his college sweetheart and another that was a very short and loveless marriage; I married my high school boyfriend, and my marriage to my second husband was quite loveless and somewhat short.
- Our birthdays are within six days of each other.
- Dick carries the traits of ADHD; my family's history of alcoholism and bipolar disorder holds similar energy.

It only took us one moment in time for our lives to intersect and for us to realize how similar our lives were. This is not to say that similarity is the only important factor in a successful relationship; however, our patterns radiated out in such a familiar fashion, it allowed us to feel comfortable with each other right off the bat. Comfort tends to allow us to feel safe, and it's the safety to be who you are that permits a relationship to flourish and succeed.

We both entered our new relationship with lots of baggage. The difference this time, in comparison to our previous relationships, is that we had both come to a point in our lives where we were now willing to accept ourselves, our strengths, and our limitations. This time we both chose to focus on our strengths while downplaying the limitations.

Through introspection, reflection, and inner child work, I have come to recognize my karmic patterns as follows: equating sickness and love; competing for love; feeling that men are weak and needy; feeling that men are just to be tolerated; having a comfort zone of feeling miserable; and feelings of superiority while at the same time having feelings of unworthiness.

Prior to meeting Dick, throughout all my familial and romantic relationships, I had been trying to run away from these feelings. I denied them. I covered them up with other feelings. I struggled against them. The truth is that you can never escape your karmic patterns. They are rooted deep within your soul. They define who you are. They are why you came to this planet. We need to learn that we cannot control or change anything. We can only surrender and accept, and in so doing, we are able to transform and create the magic that makes life simple once again.

And while we are making this miraculous transformation, we must also let go of any expected outcomes. We must let the answer come to us, rather than force it to appear on our own time line. In order to accomplish this task, we must act in self-referral and not object-referral. In other words, we must try hard not to let our ego get in the way of our spirit. The more insightful you become and the more you increase your self awareness, the better chance you have in creating opportunities that will allow you to let go of things that bring you pain and suffering.

In my instance, no one could make me feel worthy or safe enough to not constantly test the strength of my partner's love for me. These are tasks that must be accomplished within you, not outside of you. Other's validation of your worth does not make you worthy to yourself.

You must feel it, breathe it, and see it inside your soul. In other words, you must **VISUALIZE** what worthy feels like until it's a living entity that you can almost touch.

You must then positively **AFFIRM** these feelings to reinforce them in your mind, body, and spirit.

And lastly, you must **MEDITATE** or reflect in your own manner about the self-knowledge that allows you to see the world in a new light. It is through these three processes that you can connect to Spirit and alter the course of your life.

Remember it's only the emotion you assign to each life event that determines the impact it will have upon subsequent experiences. We must not let our circumstances define us. We are in charge of deciding what part they will play. Again, we must *respond* rather than *react*. Reacting creates that fight or flight response that we spoke of earlier. It causes us to act in object-referral, placing blame on others and uncontrollable circumstances, rather than accepting our own circumstances and living our life fully aware of them. As we remain in self-awareness, we must constantly be readjusting our inner compass to locate that place of balance within ourselves.

Finding the balance comes in many different forms. Each of us holds within us both male and female energy. The male energy is the 'to do' energy, while the female energy is the 'to be' energy. Part of our *karma*, or job in this lifetime, is to find the place where these two energies are in balance, both in our relationship with ourselves and in our relationships with others. Striving for balance, while recognizing the duality of our natures, is what allows for soul growth. And it is soul growth that allows us to move more toward enlightenment and to understand the difference between a response and a reaction.

Now it's very possible for you to understand all of these concepts and still not be able to apply them to your own lives. It took me years of fighting against my generational patterns to come to this place. It is only when I decided to accept myself, all of my fallibilities and insecurities, when I found the contentment for which I had been searching. I am still the same person who has made lots of mistakes and still continues to do so. The difference is that when I make a mistake now, I recognize it sooner and am able to back up quicker instead of remaining stuck in my old patterns.

Most changes come to our lives in baby steps. Sometimes they are so small it seems as if we are not progressing at all. Just the fact that you're reading this book and others like it or considering new lines of thought indicates that you are moving forward in your journey. Always remember to look over your shoulder to see where you were yesterday, a week ago, or a month ago. It will remind you that today might not be where you ultimately see yourself, but it is certainly better than where you were yesterday. Your confusion and upheaval is really a state of grace. It's only in murkiness that we can clearly recognize a stream of light trying to break through our self-imposed barriers.

Conclusion

I mentioned earlier that if you were reading this book you were drawn to it energetically, and that is exactly the concept that I have been trying to explain. Once you understand what energy is, and then are able to properly access, communicate, harness and create with it, you can begin to see the big picture of your life. Examining your childhood, you can begin to understand how generational patterns created at an early age can stifle the ability to create what we want in life and who we ultimately want to become.

It is my hope that I've inspired you to take a look at your own stuff in order to figure out why your life may not be going the way you want it to go. Perhaps, you will also walk away with a better understanding of how to take charge of your life by learning to respond to situations rather than reflexively react. Remember, none of us are perfect, but we all certainly have the potential for greatness.

I'll leave you with some simple statements in the next section that embody many of the concepts discussed throughout the book. Think of them as reminders as to how this world works and use them as frequently as you see fit to bring your life back into perspective.

Blessings to you!

Keeping Positive Energy Alive

Melind-ism's to Live By

"All events on this planet are neutral events except for the emotion we assign to them."

"It's a like-attracts-like world."

"What we resist, persists."

"If you don't go out on a limb, you can't get the fruit."

""In order to meditate, you simply close your eyes; shut your mouth; empty your mind; and breath."

"Anything can be accomplished by using the **Three Keys to Life:** ***meditation, affirmation, and visualization."***

"God is like a giant mirror, and whatever we send out to God reflects back to us in a non-judgmental way."

***"Karma is a repeat of energetic patterns and not an* eye for an eye."**

"Fear attracts and love creates."

"God is an energy force and not a being."

"We are all connected through collective consciousness."

"Never attach yourself to an outcome. This way you will never be disappointed."

"Your intentions are just as important as your actions."

"Karma can be both good and bad."

"Our life's journey is to turn our Karma to Dharma (the ultimate purpose for your incarnation)."

"Never stand too long in the shadow of one teacher."

"Use your intuition. If something doesn't feel right, it probably isn't."

"You can have the best of intentions and the worst of outcomes."

"Life is always about learning."

"If we were perfect, we wouldn't be on this planet. Our job would be done."

"The way we communicate with the outside world was learned from watching our parent's interactions with each other; our interactions with them, and our interactions with siblings, if you have any."

"Surrender to your emotions to release them."

"You create your own reality."

"Your reality is a reflection of you."

"Journal your emotions in order to learn from them."

"The male energy is the 'to do' energy. The female energy is the 'to be' energy."

"You must respond instead of react to negativity in your life."

"Guilt is a useless emotion."

"There are two core emotions on this planet: love and fear."

"There are no coincidences."

"Always look for synchronicities."

"We are all multidimensional beings who are constantly exchanging energy with everything we come into contact with."

"All of our lives run concurrently at the same time."

"We are all beings of energy."

"God never leaves you without an answer."